CHRISTMAS COUNTDOWN

STEVE ENGLEHART has written for both kids and adults throughout his career, in a variety of media. He was the last lead writer for *Marvel Comics* during their ascendancy, and later wrote the Batman stories that inspired the 1989 movie. His first novel, *The Point Man*, won praise from critics and readers alike, and research for a second, set in the Silicon Valley, led him to the computer industry as a game designer. But while all that was going on, he and his wife, Terry, produced two sons, which led him to focus more on tales for children. A companion book to *Christmas Countdown*, entitled *Easter Parade*, will be published by Avon Camelot.

BRYNA WALDMAN studied art in New York City but has moved to the more serene Oregon woods from which she receives her inspiration. She makes her home with two cats.

CHRISTMAS COUNTDOWN

STEVE ENGLEHART

Illustrated by Bryna Waldman

AN AVON CAMELOT BOOK

CHRISTMAS COUNTDOWN is an original publication of Avon Books. This work has never before appeared in book form.

AVON BOOKS
A division of
The Hearst Corporation
1350 Avenue of the Americas
New York, New York 10019

Library of Congress Cataloging in Publication Data:

Englehart, Steve.
    Christmas countdown/Steve Englehart: illustrations by Bryna
Waldman.
        p.   cm.
    Summary: A collection of twenty-five brief readings to be read
between the first of December and Christmas exploring various
aspects of the holiday.
    1. Christmas—Juvenile literature. [1. Christmas.] I. Waldman,
Bryna, ill. II. Title.
    GT4985.E54 1992   92-19267
    394.2′68282—dc20   CIP
                                                 AC

First Avon Camelot Printing: October 1993

CAMELOT TRADEMARK REG. U.S. PAT. OFF. AND IN OTHER COUNTRIES, MARCA REGISTRADA, HECHO EN U.S.A.

Printed in the U.S.A.

ARC 10 9 8 7 6 5 4 3 2 1

To Alex and Eric,
who want to know.
S.E.

To Lonnie and Robert,
who have shown me how wonderful
Christmas can be.
B.W.

Contents

CHRISTMAS
COUNTDOWN

DECEMBER 1

Advent

Christmas is celebrated all over the world as the birthday of Jesus Christ. Nobody knows the exact date of that birthday, but it's been fixed on December 25 since A.D. 354. That day was chosen by the early church fathers because it came at the time of the winter solstice, which is when the sun, having fallen lower and lower in the sky during autumn, starts to move higher again. As you know, the first day of winter is the shortest day of the year. Since the days begin to get longer, people who worshipped other gods had joyful festivals, celebrating the "rebirth" of the sun as a sign of their gods' power. The Christians felt that that time should be reserved for their Messiah, no matter when he was born.

Since then, many families have celebrated Advent, an official church period which begins on the fourth Sunday before Christmas. This is a time to prepare for Jesus's birthday in a religious way by going to church and lighting candles on a special Advent wreath.

Less formally, many people prepare for Christmas through the whole month of December by sending Christmas cards, singing Christmas carols, decorating a Christmas tree, and going to Christmas parties. The houses and streets of their towns become brightly lit, store windows have fancy displays, and yards show scenes of Christ's birth.

Children can enjoy the custom with an Advent calendar, which has little windows to open each day in December leading up to Christmas. The exciting process of finding a new treat every day is also here in this book. By reading one chapter every night before you go to bed, or by having your parents read it to you, you'll discover the wide range of fun and interesting activities that make up the Christmas season.

DECEMBER 2

The Birth of Jesus

Two thousand years ago a woman named Mary in the town of Nazareth was visited by an angel. The angel told her that she would bear a child who would be called "the Son of the Most High; and the Lord God will give Him the throne of His father David." Mary couldn't understand this, because she wasn't yet married and because the man she was to marry was named Joseph, but the angel assured her it was true—and she accepted his word. Soon she was carrying the child.

Not quite nine months later, the Roman emperor, Caesar Augustus, who ruled Mary's and Joseph's land of Judea, ordered all men to return to their families' ancestral towns for a census. For Joseph, that meant a trip to Bethlehem. Joseph was a descendant of Bethlehem's most famous son, David, the shepherd boy who had killed Goliath one thousand years earlier and gone on to become the land's king. When Mary heard that, she finally understood the angel's prophecy about David and insisted on accompanying Joseph, even though she was very close to giving birth. She knew her baby would not be born until she arrived.

Now, Bethlehem at that time was only a small cluster of houses with just one inn. Because Mary had had to travel slowly, the young couple found the village already overflowing with other pilgrims when they arrived. There was only one place for them: the stables behind the inn. And there, in the humblest spot imaginable, the baby they named Jesus came into this world.

And this world changed forever.

DECEMBER 3

The Giving of Gifts

The birth of the Son of the Most High could not go unnoticed, even if it took place in humble and hidden surroundings far from his mother's home. First, an angel appeared to shepherds in the fields around Bethlehem to give them the good news. Then, a star appeared in the sky to excite the interest of astrologers, men who studied the stars for meaning. Many of these men, called magi, set out in the direction of this new star to learn its meaning, bearing gifts for whatever wondrous thing they might find. Three of them made their way to Bethlehem, and when they found Jesus twelve days after his birth, they presented him with gold and two kinds of precious incense, frankincense and myrrh.

Gold, of course, was as valuable then as it is today. In addition, in those days it was difficult for people to take baths; and animals, as things to eat, sell, or ride, were much more in evidence—which meant civilization did not smell as sweet as it does today. Items which perfumed the air were highly prized, and incense was a very special gift. The value of incense has diminished over time, but frankincense and myrrh are still often used in some churches because the magi gave them to Jesus. Both can be found in stores that sell incense. If you have a store like this in your town, or if your parents can buy some through mail order, you can smell today what Jesus smelled as his first gifts.

The scene of the baby Jesus, Mary and Joseph, the shepherds, magi, and animals in the stables is now a work of art often seen at Christmas. Called a crèche (the French word for "crib"), this group of figures has been made in every sort of material and in every size, from that which sits on a table to that which fills a town square.

DECEMBER 4

The Givers of Gifts

*I*n the Roman world that Jesus was born into, gifts were exchanged on New Year's Day. These were generally lamps, for light in the midwinter darkness; money, for prosperity in the new year; and baked goods, for the sweetness in life. When the date for Christmas was settled on, the custom shifted backward a week or so. Since Christ was the person being celebrated, he was said to bring the gifts, and this is still the case in parts of central Europe. In Germany the term for "little Christ child" is *Kristkindlein*—which has become over the years "Kris Kringel," a name which has lived on in the English language without any thought of Jesus.

Later, Jesus ended his personal involvement with gifts in most of the world. In Germany, he sent an emissary, Knecht Ruprecht* (knight Rupert), to give gifts to good boys and girls. But as each succeeding year took the world farther away from the joy of the actual birth, Knecht Ruprecht grew harsher toward those who weren't as good as he would have liked. His form changed to show it, and he became a sort of goblin, known as Pelznickel, the "furry elf." Pelznickel came during the first week in December to judge whether children would even *have* a Christmas. He became so terrifying, especially for young children, that another messenger, a beautiful woman dressed in white, came on Christmas Eve to reprieve those Pelznickel had condemned and give them their Christmas and their gifts.

But it would fall to someone else to tame Pelznickel completely. When that time came, just a few centuries ago, the elf had become known throughout Europe as Black Peter—and the person who tamed him was jolly old Saint Nicholas!

More tomorrow on the man who became Santa Claus.

---

*"Knecht" is pronounced "K-necht," almost like "connect."

DECEMBER 5

Saint Nicholas

*A*round the year 300, in the town of Myra, in what is now the country of Turkey, there lived a bishop of the young Christian church called Nikola. To this day he is one of the youngest men to become a bishop—so young he was known as the "boy bishop." One day a man came to Nikola. The man had three daughters, all of whom wanted to marry at the same time, and he was obligated to give each of them money to help them begin their marriages. But the man didn't earn enough to do that, so he asked Bishop Nikola to loan him money. The church itself was poor, and Nikola said he couldn't do it.

In fact, Nikola *wanted* to help the man and his daughters. He just didn't want everyone to know about it, because then everyone would ask him for a loan. That night, after everyone else in the village was asleep, he secretly climbed to the man's rooftop and dropped three bags of gold down his chimney.

When Nikola kept on doing things like that, Myra became famous as a "village blessed by God." The ships that stopped there on their way across the Greek empire carried the tale to the emperor Diocletian, who didn't like the church. Since Nikola was head of the church in Myra, Diocletian had Nikola arrested. As Diocletian expected, the secret giving stopped.

Nikola spent ten years in jail, until Diocletian was replaced by Constantine, an emperor who supported the church. He released Nikola, and the bishop returned to Myra. The gifts began appearing again, so people became certain that Nikola was the giver, but even then he retained his modesty. In the English language, we call him Saint Nicholas, and tomorrow, December 6, we'll learn how Saint Nicholas became Santa Claus.

DECEMBER 6

The Feast of Saint Nicholas

In the Catholic Church, men and women who have lived truly Christian lives can be designated as saints. Each saint has a special day set aside for his or her celebration, and for Saint Nicholas—Bishop Nikola of Myra—it is the day he died, December 6. Nicholas became a saint not only because he was a good man, but also because the stories of his generosity lived after him. Though he had nothing to do with Christmas originally, over time the Christian gift giver became first tied to the Christian gift-giving season. It may be confusing to us for Saint Nick to have two days to make his rounds, but having two chances to give gifts must be pleasing to *him*.

Just as with Christmas, the celebration of St. Nicholas's Day begins the night before, on St. Nicholas's Eve. Before they go to bed, children put their shoes by the fireplace or on a window ledge outside their houses, and fill the shoes with hay for the saint's beautiful white horse. They also leave a saucer of water for the horse, though that usually freezes if they leave it outside. Late at night, after everyone's gone to sleep, Nicholas rides up on a cart full of presents. Because on St. Nicholas's Eve he retains his role as a bishop, Nicholas wears a bishop's red hat and cape. He also has complete control over the bad-tempered elf, Black Peter, who rides with him. Very bad children can expect only a stick from Black Peter, but most children earn Nicholas's rewards. He lets his horse eat the hay out of the shoes, and then fills them with presents and cookies.

Saint Nicholas is especially popular in Holland, and at noon on December 6, he comes back to that country in a boat. When the boat docks, he rides ashore on his white horse, and a grand celebration begins for the man the Dutch call Sint Nicolaas . . . or . . . Sinter Klaas.

DECEMBER 7

Christmas in America

You might think that Christmas has always been popular, but this isn't true—not even here in America. The Puritans, Quakers, Presbyterians, Methodists, and Baptists—all of whom had broken away from the Catholic Church—felt that as a Catholic remnant of a pagan festival for the sun god, Christmas was a false holiday. The Puritans who landed at Plymouth Rock in December 1620 deliberately built a house on Christmas Day. In 1647, the Puritans in England outlawed both Christmas and Easter, and from 1659 to 1681 their American cousins fined anyone caught celebrating Christmas.

On the other hand, the Catholics, Anglicans, Episcopalians, German Lutherans, and Dutch Reformed members celebrated the Christmas season enthusiastically—which meant, in the Dutchmen's case, celebrating St. Nicholas Day on December 6. Even though others chose December 25 for their celebration, the Dutch staged the most joyous festivities, so that soon all Americans, whether they paid attention to him or not, came to know Saint Nicholas by his Dutch name, Sinter Klaas—which eventually became Santa Claus.

The conflicts over celebrating or not celebrating, and when to celebrate, went on for nearly 250 years. George Washington crossed the Delaware River on Christmas night, 1776, and surprised the Hessian soldiers who were celebrating rather than standing guard. When church and state were officially separated by the American Constitution in 1791, opposition on religious grounds started to fade. But it wasn't until the late 1860s that distrust of Christmas was finally put to rest throughout America, and December 25 became the date we celebrate.

DECEMBER 8

Our Santa Claus

*I*n the year 1003, Czar Vladimir of Russia went to Turkey for his baptism, and was so taken by the stories of Saint Nicholas there that he made Nicholas the patron saint of Russia. (Nicholas is also the patron saint of Greece, Sicily, sailors, and children.) The saint's fame spread from Russia to the other northlands, and from then on he was as likely to be seen with reindeer as with his white horse. His home became the North Pole.

England adopted him and called him Father Christmas. France gave him the same name, Père Noël. But it was an American, Clement Clarke Moore, who first described the Santa Claus we know today, in his famous poem "A Visit from St. Nicholas." Written in 1822, with its immortal opening line "'Twas the Night before Christmas . . ." it forever changed the Turkish bishop into a jolly fat elf. For the first time we heard of a sleigh drawn by eight reindeer called Dasher and Dancer and Prancer and Vixen and Comet and Cupid and Donder and Blitzen. For the first time we heard that Santa wore fur and carried a sack of toys on his back. For the first time we heard about his merry face and white beard and small pipe.

The poem became an instant classic, but still, we had only *heard* about Santa. It was some forty years later, in 1863, that a famous cartoonist named Thomas Nast *showed* us how he really looked. Nast's drawings over the next twenty-five years came to define the Santa we all recognize today. Nast also showed us Santa's workshop at the North Pole and all his elfin helpers.

But Santa Claus, though a major part of the Christmas season, is only a part, and starting tomorrow we'll have a look at all the other parts—beginning with the festive greenery we use to decorate our own Christmas world.

DECEMBER 9

Christmas Plants

*E*ven though Christmas takes place in the depths of winter, it celebrates the light that never dies. That's why evergreens, which don't shed their leaves like most trees, and plants that recall the summer are part of the celebration.

The most famous Christmas flower is the poinsettia. It was long known to the Central and South Americans as *La Flor de Noche Buena*, "the flower of the Good Night" (the Good Night is their name for Christmas Eve). Dr. Joel Poinsett first saw it in 1828 and brought it into the United States in 1836, which is how it got its American name. Its colors of green and red are the traditional Christmas colors: green for the undying evergreen and red for the blood of Jesus, to remind us he was born and lived and died like any other man.

The most famous Christmas plant is mistletoe. Mistletoe generally grows high up on oak trees, without ever putting its own roots in the ground. For that reason, the druids of ancient Britain thought the oak transferred its life force into the mistletoe to hold during the time the oak had no leaves. This close relationship between the two led the druids to think of the close relationship between men and women, so mistletoe boughs held high in the air allowed men and women to kiss underneath. Just be sure never to eat any mistletoe berries, because they are very poisonous.

After mistletoe has been cut from an oak, it begins to turn golden. Its brightest color comes after six months. So mistletoe cut in midsummer and used at midwinter seemed to bring the bright summer sunlight to the Yuletide's darkness.

DECEMBER 10

Evergreens

A number of evergreens are linked to Christmas. Next to the Christmas tree itself, the best known evergreen is holly. Holly means "holy," and for centuries in England *it* was called "Christmas tree." Holly has two types of leaves: thorny ones representing men, and smooth ones representing women. English tradition says that the first type brought into the house after Advent showed who would rule the house in the coming year—which led to a lot of races between men and women! Holly's shiny green leaves are highlighted by bright red berries, so a wreath made of holly sets the perfect mood at Christmas.

The other traditional evergreens are:

Ivy—dedicated to love because it clings. Perhaps because holly can be separated into two sexes and ivy seeks to close any gaps, holly and ivy are reputed to fight with each other. A fifteenth century carol says holly's holiness wins out over ivy's love, but in fact, holiness and love go together better than the carolers pretended.

Rosemary—used as an incense, as well as a flavoring for almost every type of food. Rosemary harkens back to the earliest days of the newborn Jesus; it's said its flowers were once white, but turned blue after Mary draped her blue cloak over the plant on the family's way out of Bethlehem. Christmas always reminds us of all the years people have gathered together at this time and of all the people we've gathered with. "There's rosemary," wrote Shakespeare, "that's for remembrance."

Box—a shrub used to create hedges. Perhaps because hedges mark off individual spaces, box represents Jesus's time on earth. English tradition calls for all other evergreens to be removed from the house soon after the New Year, but box stays up until Easter, when Jesus's time here ended.

DECEMBER 11

The Christmas Tree

There are many evergreens, but the pine or fir remains the most enduring symbol of the Christmas season. Long before the time of Christ, these trees were the symbol of immortality to the peoples of the Mediterranean, not only because their needles stayed green all year, but also because their shape pointed toward heaven. Fir, which is a member of the pine family, was sacred in Greece to Artemis, the mother-goddess; her symbol was an ivy-twined, fir-cone–tipped branch.

One old story says that when Mary, Joseph, and Jesus were fleeing Bethlehem and the king's soldiers, the family hid in the hollow trunk of a huge pine tree. After the soldiers had ridden past, Jesus blessed the pine. Nowadays, if you cut a pine cone in half lengthwise, you'll see the shape of his hand.

Because people had worshipped nature, and most particularly trees, before the birth of Jesus, all decorations using pine, fir, holly, and the other plants were strictly forbidden by the church until the Middle Ages. One story has it that Martin Luther, a German church leader in the early 1500s who fought and eventually broke away from the Catholic Church, saw brilliant stars one winter's night and was reminded of the stars over Bethlehem. He decided to cut down a fir tree and take it home so it could hold the starlike lights of candles. But the first Christmas tree we truly know about existed in 1604, nearly sixty years after Luther's death, in the German town of Strassburg. Christmas trees soon became the centerpiece of German celebrations, and the custom spread from there to the rest of continental Europe and America. Christmas trees reached America long before they reached England. It wasn't until after Germany's Prince Albert married England's Queen Victoria in 1840 that her country adopted the Christmas tree.

DECEMBER 12

Decorating the Tree

Trees live much longer than people and so, to the ancients, seemed godlike. Well, if a tree standing in the woods was a god, wouldn't it enjoy being brought into a person's house and honored? The ancients soon decided that the more examples of continuing life they could hang on the tree, the more likely it was that the god would understand what they wanted. These people used candles, fruits, paper flowers, cakes shaped like animals, and pictures of their gods.

When trees became part of the Christmas celebration after the Puritan era, these same ideas were brought back. New decorations were added, including strings of popcorn and bright red cranberries, colorful painted nuts, handmade ornaments, candies, and cookies. Candles came to be placed on little stands with colored paper behind them or colored glass in front of them, to provide different colors of light. But candles were always watched closely and extinguished after a short time, since candles on a tree can much too easily start a fire. Once electric light bulbs became available, they quickly replaced the open flames.

A special decoration is often placed on the very top of the tree, the part closest to heaven. Sometimes it's a star, like the star of Bethlehem. Sometimes it's a beautiful angel, looking down at us as the first angels looked down over Jesus.

Other countries have their own customs for decoration, and as people have learned more about their neighbors in the world, they added those customs to their own. Ornaments like marzipan fruits from Europe, origami birds from Japan, and straw figures from South America can give a Christmas tree an international look—a good reminder that this season is a time for the fellowship of all people, all over the world.

DECEMBER 13

The Feast of St. Lucia

Today is another saint's day, and another day for presents to be exchanged in some parts of Europe. The beautiful St. Lucia is as famous and honored in Scandinavia and Sicily as St. Nicholas is in Holland. In the southern tip of Italy, a young non-Christian woman named Lucia was about to be married, and her father had given her money. However, she admired Christians so much that she gave her money to the church instead of to her fiancé. Angered, the young man denounced her to the authorities as a witch, and Lucia was ordered burned at the stake. But when the fire was lit, it refused to touch her, and she had to be killed with a sword.

The name "Lucia" means "woman of light"—specifically the light of dawn. Of course, dawn is the birth time of the day, and long ago, when the calendar wasn't as carefully calculated as it is now, December 13 was thought to be the day of the winter solstice, when the whole year is "born." So some people argue that this festival celebrates only light and has nothing to do with the saint.

Either way, this day is very important in Sweden and other parts of Scandinavia, as well as in parts of America with many Scandinavian-Americans. The youngest girl in the house gets up before dawn and puts on a white dress with a red sash and a crown made of branches from the bilberry bush (similar to the cranberry). This crown traditionally holds several candles, though today small flashlights provide the same light more safely. She goes through the house or the neighborhood as the sun is rising, waking everyone up and giving them something to drink. In some places she's accompanied by maids of honor and "star boys." Everyone they meet knows that light has come back to the world.

DECEMBER 14

The Yule Log

The most impressive symbol of light at Christmas is the Yule log. This is a piece of wood picked out in the summertime so that it's well seasoned and ready to burn when Christmas comes. Usually cut from an oak, the Yule log should be the largest hunk of wood that can fit into the fireplace. In the days before furnaces, fireplaces often took up half a wall, but these days the fireplace and the log are smaller. Whatever its size, the Yule log should have an interesting shape. Stumps with gnarled roots are especially prized. The log is pushed as far into the hearth as possible, where it is lit with a remnant of last year's log. After it burns, a chunk of the log is kept to light next year's log. These remnants are also charms against fire, so they're guarded closely throughout the year.

The custom comes from Scandinavia, where the ancient pagans worshipped Odin and believed that the universe was held up by a great tree called Yggdrasil. When Christianity set out to win over these people, the priests convinced them to burn a huge log representing Yggdrasil. This showed their acceptance of Jesus as the Light of the World. "Yule" comes from the Scandinavian word *iul*, meaning "wheel." The traditional twelve days of Christmas represent the twelve months of the year, which is how long it takes the earth to wheel around the sun.

Later, the custom of the Yule log spread to other parts of Europe, and England took it on wholeheartedly. The English revel consisted of the entire family (and servants, if any) dragging the log back to the house through the woods. Along the way they sang special songs and played special games. Once the log was in the house, each person sat on it and kissed it. Then the oldest member of the family poured wine on the log to "baptize" it, before it was set aflame. As it filled the room with light and warmth, the family feasting began.

DECEMBER 15

Food and Drink

A great tradition in foods has grown up around Christmas.

Before the meal, some grown-ups drink from a special wassail bowl. "Wassail" comes from *waes heill*, meaning "be well," or (in a more modern manner) "cheers!" The wassail bowl had evergreen branches attached to its sides and tied together above so it could be carried from guest to guest, and was filled with specially spiced ale or wine. If toasted apples, cream, and eggs were added, the drink was called "lambswool," because it was so smooth. Eggnog is a modern variation on lambswool.

Though rarely eaten anymore, *the* traditional food for an English Christmas was the head of a boar, or pig. King Henry VIII established that custom in the early 1500s, and his boar's heads were flavored with rosemary and bay. But boar has always been hard for average people to find, so first the Christmas goose took its place, and then the Christmas turkey. Turkeys are native to North America and didn't exist in Europe until they were taken back there by early explorers. By the 1600s they were well established as a centerpiece of Christmas on both continents.

Plum pudding originated at the same time. It started out as plum porridge—a goopy mix of fruit, spices, bread, and meat broth—which had been cooked an extra length of time to make it more solid. The fruit probably was plums in the beginning, but it soon became raisins, even though the name didn't change. Remember Little Jack Horner? While "eating his Christmas pie/ He put in his thumb/And pulled out a plum . . ."

Mince pie, also originally including meat but nowadays generally made entirely of fruit, comes from the same porridge.

DECEMBER 16

Las Posadas

On this day, the Latin American world begins its ten-day Christmas festival called *las Posadas*, which runs right through to Christmas day. *Las Posadas* means "the inns," because every night a procession of celebrants "searches for lodgings for Mary and Joseph." These people go from house to house (or room to room if only one house is involved) asking for shelter, but are continually turned away. Finally, one place admits them, and then prayers are said. After that, the adults relax and enjoy a meal. And this happens every night for ten days!

But the children's favorite part of the festival involves the piñata, a jar originally made out of clay but now more often made of papier-mâché. The piñata is decorated with crepe paper and hung from the ceiling or a doorway. The children of the house or the neighborhood gather underneath the piñata and one of them is blindfolded; that one is given a stick and three tries at whacking the piñata. If the piñata remains unbroken, the next child gets a chance, and so on until someone gets lucky. Since hitting something you can't see isn't easy it usually takes a while, but the wait is worth it because when the piñata breaks it spills out everything that was inside it—toys and candy. As soon as those things start falling, the children—even the one with the blindfold on—scramble to gather whatever they can.

Mexican homes during *las Posadas* are decorated with the same evergreens and poinsettias we use, but they also enjoy white lilies.

DECEMBER 17

Christmas Cards

*T*he only one of our Christmas traditions that doesn't reach back to antiquity is the sending of Christmas cards. This is because there was no way to send them until the modern post office came into being.

In the early 1800s, English schoolboys were required to write letters to their parents before Christmas, demonstrating their penmanship. These letters often covered a subject on the boys' minds: the Christmas presents they hoped to receive. Some enterprising businessman began to sell special forms for these letters, decorated around the edges with Christmas pictures. But these were still not Christmas cards as we know them.

In 1843, Henry Cole was a British government employee charged with improving the post office. He conceived the idea of an actual Christmas card and had a friend design it. The result was not a great success. It took five years before another card appeared, but thereafter the business slowly increased. In 1870, postcards were created and given a stamp half the price of a letter's. Coupled with advances in cheap printing, Christmas cards blossomed.

In America they continued to be rare, however. Then in 1875, Louis Prang of Boston began selling beautifully designed cards which quickly became the thing to give. He reproduced oil paintings, printed "Merry Christmas" across the top, and within five years was selling five million cards a year. But in 1890, less expensive and less elegant cards were imported from Germany, undercutting Prang's market so completely that he soon gave up Christmas cards altogether.

Since that time, Christmas cards have become more and more prevalent. They have become a wonderful way to keep in touch with all your friends from the entire year.

DECEMBER 18

Christmas Carols

Singing has always been one way of showing joy, and joy is all around at Christmas. In early times, Christmas songs were sung only in church, and these songs were in Latin, the official church language. This meant that ordinary people couldn't express their joy very easily. So in the 1200s, ordinary people began to make up their own songs. They gathered together outside the church to sing them, and created what the French called "carols," meaning "to sing and dance in a ring." Originally, there were carols for all the major church holidays, but by the 1600s carols became concentrated at Christmas alone.

When the Puritans took power they outlawed carols, just as they outlawed everything they disapproved of. But since carols existed outside the church, they were much harder to control. People gathered in their homes as they always had, and sang. For one hundred years carols existed only in hearts and minds.

In the 1700s, night watchmen, men who walked through the neighborhoods after dark making sure everything was all right, began to sing and play instruments on their rounds. After a time, regular musicians found that joining them at Christmas was a good way to advance their careers, and they recalled some of the old songs. But another hundred years went by before an Englishman named Davies Gilbert gathered up what songs he could and published a *Collection of Christmas Carols* in 1822. Soon other people across Europe gathered their own local songs, and carols became readily available again. For the next forty years, carols remained in danger of being discarded as remnants of the past, but by the 1860s, it was clear that they were here to stay.

DECEMBER 19

Christmas Performances

Since the earliest days of the church, reenactments of the birth of Jesus have been staged. Nativity plays became more and more elaborate over the centuries, especially in the Middle Ages, but simple versions will never go out of style because simplicity is the hallmark of the story.

The greatest of Christmas music performances is the *Messiah*, composed in 1741 by George Frederick Handel, a German who became an English citizen. In addition to his work as a composer, he was a governor at an orphanage, where he performed *Messiah* every year. These performances actually occurred more often at Easter than at Christmas, but the ties to the joys of children soon tied *Messiah* to this season.

Charles Dickens wrote *A Christmas Carol* in 1843, the same year that Henry Cole created the Christmas card. The story gained popularity because Dickens truly loved Christmas and used many of its most beloved aspects in his tale. The story of Ebenezer Scrooge and the three ghosts who taught him that Christmas means love has never gone out of fashion.

The classic Christmas ballet, *The Nutcracker*, was composed in 1892 by Pyotr Ilich Tchaikovsky, a Russian. This story of childhood dreams was not popular when first presented, possibly because ballets weren't often attended by children, but the music alone quickly won the world over.

The most modern of the now-traditional performances is *Amahl and the Night Visitors*, an opera written for television in 1951. Gian Carlo Menotti's story tells of Amahl, a crippled shepherd boy, whose mother gives shelter to the magi and receives the miracle of Amahl's healing.

DECEMBER 20

Christmas Legends

As each Christmas has come around, year after year for nearly 2,000 years, a number of legends have endured.

- Children born on Christmas have the power to see and command spirits. These spirits give them the gift of prophecy.

- Bread baked on Christmas will never become moldy.

- Roosters crow all night long on Christmas Eve, proclaiming not the usual coming of the dawn, but the coming of the Light of the World.

- The cow in the stables warmed the baby Jesus with her breath, and that's why a cow's breath is sweeter than any other animal's.

- All the animals who were in the stables—the cow and the horse and the donkey—kneel at midnight on Christmas Eve.

- All the animals in the world can speak then, but it's very unlucky for any person to hear them.

- Trees burst into blossom that same night. Joseph of Arimathea, the man who provided Jesus with a burial place, went to England in later life. There on a Christmas Eve, he thrust his hawthorn-wood staff into the ground at a holy place called Glastonbury, and it turned into a tree which blossomed every Christmas Eve thereafter. That tree was cut down when the Puritans were in power, but hawthorn is a strong tree, and new growths soon appeared. Cuttings from them were planted elsewhere, and carry on the tradition. (A cutting from one of the daughter trees was planted in Washington, D.C. in 1902, and has blossomed there on Christmas Eve since 1918.)

DECEMBER 21

The Winter Solstice

Today is the shortest day of the year. Darkness fills much of our time now, and the chill of winter forces us to stay inside, yet everything we do seems brighter than at any other time of the year. That is the magic of Christmas—but why is it so dark?

The earth travels around the sun once a year, but it doesn't travel in a circle. Instead, it moves in an ellipse, which is the same shape as an egg. At one point during the year, it is closer to the sun than at any other time, and at another point, is farther away. These two points are called the solstices. You might guess that the earth is farthest away right now, but you'd be wrong. The winter solstice is the closer point. Then, why is it cold?

It's cold because the equator, the imaginary line around the center of the earth, doesn't point directly at the sun. The earth, in fact, is tilted in relation to the sun, and right now, the earth's northern half is tilted away from the sun. That's what makes the northern half darker and colder. But as the earth moves on around its ellipse, the northern half turns more and more toward the sun, until we reach the heat of the summer solstice in June—when we're farthest away from the sun.

But what about the southern half of the earth? Well, right now, South America and Australia are having their summer heat, even though it's Christmastime for them, too. Kids are out of school, not for their Christmas break, but for their regular summer vacation. For many years, Australians on Christmas favored the traditional hot meal of England, but in recent years cold cuts have become the lunch of choice, particularly since families often celebrate with a picnic at the beach.

DECEMBER 22

Hanging Stockings

On St. Nicholas's Day in Holland, children put their shoes out for St. Nicholas to fill with presents. Most of the children in Europe, though, as well as the children in America, hang stockings. Some European children hang them beside their windows on St. Andrew's Eve, the beginning of Advent on November 29. But most people hang them by the chimney, in preparation for December 25. In most of the Northern Hemisphere, remember, stockings that are worn on the feet are likely to be cold and wet from snow, so hanging them near the fire is a very logical custom.

Today, of course, we rarely use the stockings we wear on our feet. Most people—grown-ups as well as children—hang specially made stockings, often decorated with their names or small pictures of Christmas.

Stocking presents are, by their very nature, small. In the 1500s, they always came in bundles of three, tied together. One present had to be useful in work, one had to make the receiver think, and one was just for fun. But if the receiver had been especially bad, all he would find was a lump of coal—a "gift" from Pelznickel! This is a custom we're glad to have lost.

But whatever presents Santa is going to bring you, your family, and friends this Christmas, the presents that you give are even more important. If you haven't finished making or buying what you want to give, this is the time to figure out what you have left to do, and then make sure it's done.

As Bishop Nikola taught his townspeople long ago, the best presents come from the heart. Little or big, it doesn't matter what you give, so long as it's what you *want* to give.

DECEMBER 23

The Twelve Days of Christmas

*M*any people think the twelve days of Christmas are days leading up to December 25, because so many things—shopping, parties, people coming home for the holidays—take place before the Big Day. But in fact, the twelve days begin the day *after* Christmas and run through the sixth of January.

The first working day after Christmas is known throughout the British Commonwealth as Boxing Day. This is usually the first day of Christmas, but not always. On this day people give presents (in boxes) to those who serve them, like the mailman. Do you suppose the partridge in the pear tree came in a *box*?

The second day is marked in Germany with the blessing of wine. Blessed wine is supposed to assure its owner of a good harvest (of turtle doves?).

The third day is called Childermas, and honors children (not to mention French hens). It's been observed since the fifth century.

The fourth and fifth days have no particular associations.

The sixth day is New Year's eve, and the seventh day New Year's Day.

The eighth, ninth, tenth, and eleventh days have no particular associations.

The twelfth day is known as Epiphany—the appearance of Jesus to the magi. In many parts of Europe, three men dress up and bring the last presents of the season to the children. Another custom is the twelfth cake. This is baked with a bean hidden somewhere inside it, and when people divvy it up, whoever gets the bean is named King or Queen of the Bean. That person then picks a queen or king, and the two of them are the stars of the party that follows. The night of twelfth day is Twelfth Night, and that's the end of the Christmas season.

DECEMBER 24

Christmas Eve

*I*n 1897, an eight-year-old girl's friends told her that Santa Claus didn't really exist. She decided to ask someone who knew, and wrote to *The New York Sun*. Francis Church, an editorial writer, wrote a reply that was published in the paper, and it was so exactly right that it went on to be republished every year for over half a century. He said:

Virginia, your little friends are wrong. They have been affected by the skepticism of a skeptical age. They do not believe except what they see. . . .

Yes, Virginia, there is a Santa Claus. He exists as certainly as love and generosity and devotion exist, and you know that they abound and give to your life its highest beauty and joy. Alas! how dreary would be the world if there were no Santa Claus! It would be as dreary as if there were no Virginias. There would be no child-like faith then, no poetry, no romance to make tolerable this existence. We should have no enjoyment, except in sense and sight. The eternal light with which childhood fills the world would be extinguished.

Not believe in Santa Claus! You might as well not believe in fairies! You might get your papa to hire men to watch in all the chimneys on Christmas Eve to catch Santa Claus, but even if they did not see Santa Claus coming down, what would that prove? Nobody sees Santa Claus, but that is no sign that there is no Santa Claus. The most real things in the world are those that no children or men can see. Did you ever see fairies dancing on the lawn? Of course not, but that's no proof that they are not there. Nobody can conceive all the wonders there are unseen or unseeable in the world. . . .

Is it all real? Ah, Virginia, in all this world there is nothing else real and abiding. No Santa Claus! Thank God! he lives, and he lives for ever. A thousand years from now, Virginia, nay, ten times ten thousand years from now, he will continue to make glad the heart of childhood.

DECEMBER 25

Merry

Christmas!